D0513913

salads

salads

Elsa Petersen-Schepelern

photography by Peter Cassidy

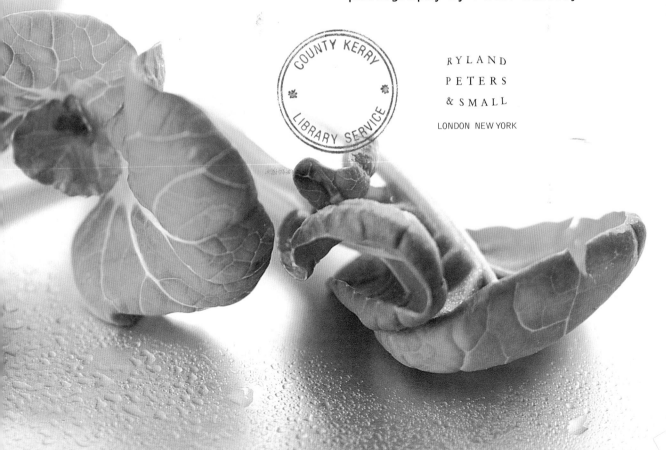

RYLAND
PETERS
& SMALL

LONDON NEW YORK

Designer Vicky Holmes

Editor Maddalena Bastianelli

Production Patricia Harrington

Art Director Gabriella Le Grazie

Publishing Director Alison Starling

Food Stylist Louise Pickford

Stylist Wei Tang

Photographer's Assistant Rachel Tomlinson

First published in Great Britain in 2001
by Ryland Peters & Small, Kirkman House,
12–14 Whitfield Street, London W1T 2RP
www.rylandpeters.com

10 9 8 7 6 5 4 3 2

Text © Elsa Petersen-Schepelern 2001
Design and photographs © Ryland Peters & Small 2001

Printed and bound in China by Toppan Printing Co.

ISBN 1 84172 113 1

A CIP record for this book is available from the British Library.

Author's acknowledgements

My thanks to my sister Kirsten, my nephews Peter Bray and Luc Votan (for his expert advice on
Vietnamese food), my cousins in Italy, Nowelle, Clemente and Tina Valentino-Capezza, to Sheridan
Lear the 'Preserving Princess', to Erica Marcus for her wise advice, and Susan Stuck, Maggie
Ramsay and Maddie Bastianelli, as ever. Halcyon Herbs provided the incredible salad leaves and
herbs – to them, my heartfelt thanks. Thanks also to the brilliant Louise Pickford for her light touch
with food styling, to Vicky Walters, to photographer Peter Cassidy who just takes my breath away, to
Wei Tang and her deft eye for styling and to Vicky Holmes for her beautiful design.

Notes

All spoon measurements are level unless otherwise noted. Ovens should be preheated to the
specified temperature. Recipes in this book were tested with a fan-assisted oven. If using a
regular oven, increase the cooking times according to the manufacturer's instructions.

contents

there's more to salads than just green...

Salads mean summer – and winter too. In this book, I have given a choice of salads for all seasons and occasions: for a light snack or a substantial meal, to serve as a starter, or as a palate cleanser between the main course and the cheese. There's even a fruit salad to serve at the end of a meal.

A salad is the sort of thing I like to take to work: homemade is always nicer, cheaper and fresher than the sort you buy from lunch bars.

The dressing makes a huge difference to a salad. I'm a great fan of simple vinaigrettes — preferably mostly oil and very little vinegar. Experiment with oils: try assertively flavoured extra virgin olive oils from different regions — or nut oils such as walnut, hazelnut or macadamia (you may need to mellow their flavours with a mild olive oil) and then there are the seed oils, such as pumpkin or sesame, which can be very strong indeed and should be used like a seasoning rather than a dressing. The same might be said for balsamic vinegar — use just a few drops, not a heavy hand.

The choice of vinegars or citrus juices depends very much on personal taste. I usually choose either mild white rice vinegar or the complex flavours of vinegars made from sherry or cider. Lemon is the smoothest of the citrus juices, lime more fragrant, and orange of course sweeter. Whatever the acidic component, I prefer it to be minimal, in a ratio of 5 or 6 parts oil to 1 of vinegar. If you need to put sugar in a vinaigrette, you've probably used too much vinegar.

Try spicy dressings from South-east Asia, flavour-packed pesto or unctuous mayonnaise. It's really no trouble to make your own fresh mayonnaise, and the ingredients are very simple – unlike store-bought versions, which always taste too vinegary, too sweet, too chemical. Give me homemade every time.

...though green is a good place to start! Salads can be cold or cool, warm or hot, but they should always include a delicious combination of various flavours, textures and colours.

LEAVES AND HERBS

Caesar salad

Classic Caesar Salad includes either a raw or 1-minute egg, but this is out of bounds for many people these days. Instead, I make it with a soft-boiled 4-minute egg. My idea of 4 minutes is timed from when the water starts to boil. If you would prefer a hard-boiled egg, by all means cook it a little longer – just 2 minutes more will make it hard-boiled.

1 small head young cos lettuce, leaves separated

2 tablespoons extra virgin olive oil

½ tablespoon freshly squeezed lemon juice, plus 1 lemon, cut into wedges

sea salt flakes and freshly ground black pepper

CROUTONS

1 thick slice challah bread, brioche or white bread

about 2 tablespoons oil and/or butter, for frying

1 large garlic clove, smashed

TO SERVE

3–4 anchovy fillets, preferably salt-packed, rinsed

1 soft-cooked (1-minute or 4-minute) egg, peeled and halved or quartered

Parmesan cheese, shaved into curls with a vegetable peeler

SERVES 1

To make the croutons, toast the slice of bread or brioche lightly on both sides. Cut into big cubes, cutting off and discarding the crusts first.

Heat the oil and/or butter in a frying pan and add the garlic. Add the cubes of bread and cook, turning frequently, until golden on all sides. Discard the garlic after about 1 minute - do not let it burn. When the cubes are golden, remove and drain on kitchen paper.

Put the lettuce leaves in a large bowl and sprinkle with the olive oil. Using your hands, roll the leaves in the oil. Sprinkle with lemon juice and roll again.

Put the croutons into a bowl and put the dressed leaves on top. Sprinkle with salt and lots of freshly ground black pepper. Add the anchovies, egg and shavings of Parmesan and serve.

Note: If you don't like anchovies, omit them, and add 1 teaspoon Worcestershire sauce or a pinch of salt with the olive oil.

Green salad

Any book on salads must include a classic green salad. I think you must stick with green – have no truck with tomatoes and peppers and things of that nature. Choose a combination of leaves – some crisp, some bitter, some peppery, some soft. The perfection of the dressing is what's important. My view is that the oil must be as marvellous as possible and the vinegar as little as possible. I also prefer it without mustard or garlic, but please yourself.

leaves from 2 small heads Little Gem lettuce, separated

leaves from 1 head chicory (witloof)

1 bag rocket, about 50 g

1 bag wild rocket, about 50 g

1 small bag watercress sprigs, trimmed, about 75 g

your choice of other leaves, such as young dandelion leaves, young nasturtium leaves, young flat leaf parsley

DRESSING

½ garlic clove (optional)

a pinch of sea salt flakes

6 parts extra virgin olive oil

1 part vinegar, such as white rice, sherry, white or red wine, or cider

1 teaspoon Dijon mustard (optional)

freshly ground black pepper

SERVES 4–6

Wash the leaves as necessary and spin dry in a salad spinner. Put in plastic bags and chill for at least 30 minutes to make the leaves crisp. (If washing soft leaves like rocket, do it at the last minute, otherwise they will go mushy - thankfully, my supermarket sells them in bags, already washed and dried.)

If using garlic, put it on a board with a pinch of sea salt and crush thoroughly with the back of a heavy knife (use a garlic crusher if you must, but I think the texture is better this way). Transfer to a salad bowl, add the olive oil, vinegar, mustard, if using, and pepper, then beat with a fork or small whisk.

When ready to serve, add the leaves and, using your hands, turn them gently in the dressing until lightly coated. (I prefer to use my hands - they don't bruise the leaves and you can make sure everything is well coated.)

Note: A few tablespoons of dressing is plenty for a salad of this size - too much will spoil it. I prefer the vinegar to be as gentle as possible. (White rice vinegar is my current favourite).

Tatsoi, avocado and frisée
with croutons and pancetta

1 bag tatsoi or other small leaves, about 75 g

1 frisée (curly endive), leaves separated

6 thin slices smoked pancetta or bacon

1 ripe Hass avocado

½ tablespoon olive oil, for frying

CROUTONS

2 garlic cloves, crushed

6 thick slices white bread

clarified butter or olive oil, for frying

DRESSING

6 tablespoons extra virgin olive oil

1 tablespoon sherry vinegar or rice vinegar

½ garlic clove, crushed

a few drops of balsamic vinegar

sea salt and freshly ground black pepper

SERVES 4

Tatsoi is a crisp baby Chinese leaf sold in many supermarkets. It's like a mini bok choy leaf — you may find it in the stir-fry vegetable section. It's good in stir-fries, but even better as a salad leaf. If you can't find it, use watercress. Balsamic vinegar is a terrific ingredient, but I think most people use too much of it. Use just a few drops to contrast with the creaminess of avocado, which in turn should be scooped out with a teaspoon — when sliced, it loses much of its appeal. This salad is delicious as a first course.

Wash the tatsoi and frisée leaves and dry in a salad spinner. Put in a plastic bag and chill.

To make the croutons, rub the garlic over the bread. Remove the crusts and cut the bread into cubes. Heat the butter or oil in a frying pan, add the bread and cook until light brown. Drain on kitchen paper.

Heat a frying pan, brush with the ½ tablespoon olive oil, add the pancetta and cook at a medium-high heat, without disturbing the pancetta, until crisp on one side. Using tongs, turn the slices over and fry until the other side is crisp. Remove and drain on kitchen paper, then cut into 5 cm lengths.

Put the dressing ingredients in a salad bowl and beat with a fork or small whisk. When ready to serve, add the leaves and turn in the dressing, using your hands. Cut the avocado in half and remove the stone. Using a teaspoon, scoop out balls of avocado into the salad. Add the crispy pancetta or bacon and serve.

Blue cheese salad
with crispy bacon and pine nuts

This salad of herb sprigs and mixed leaves – peppery, soft and bitter – is dressed with a creamy blue cheese dressing. I often serve it at weekday dinner parties because it covers three courses in one; first, salad and cheese.

2 tablespoons pine nuts

1 tablespoon olive oil, for frying

8–12 slices smoked streaky bacon or pancetta

125 g dolcelatte, Gorgonzola or other blue cheese, diced

3 tablespoons extra virgin olive oil, or to taste

1 tablespoon white rice vinegar or freshly squeezed lemon juice, or to taste

mixed salad leaves, including peppery leaves like watercress and mustard, bitter ones like frisée, soft ones like mignonette or butter lettuce, and herb sprigs like rocket

1 Hass avocado, scooped into balls with a teaspoon (optional)

sea salt flakes and freshly ground black pepper

SERVES 4

Put the pine nuts in a dry frying pan and sauté for about 1-2 minutes only, until golden - shake and stir several times to prevent burning. Set aside.

Heat the olive oil in the pan, add the pancetta or bacon and fry until crisp. Transfer to a plate lined with kitchen paper to drain.

Put the cheese in a large salad bowl and crumble well with a fork. Add the extra virgin olive oil and vinegar or lemon juice. Mash, then beat to a loose and creamy consistency, adding water if necessary - alternatively, use a hand-held blender. Add salt and lots of freshly ground black pepper to taste.

Put the salad leaves on top of the cheese dressing, then add the avocado, if using. Sprinkle with the pancetta and pine nuts (scrape any crunchy bits from the pan into the bowl too).

Serve, in the salad bowl, for guests to help themselves, or make in 4 separate bowls, dividing the ingredients as appropriate. Lots of wine and crusty bread are perfect accompaniments.

This version of the famous salad was taught to me by a Lebanese doctor, a frequent visitor to London, who is most particular about his tabbouleh. The most important thing to remember is that this is a parsley and mint salad, not a bulgar wheat or couscous salad. There should be so much green that you hardly notice the grain — or the tomatoes.

Lebanese tabbouleh

Soak the bulgar wheat in water for 20 minutes, then drain. Skin, deseed and chop the tomatoes, then chop the parsley and mint.

Put the tomatoes, herbs, spring onions and bulgar wheat in a bowl. Sprinkle with the olive oil and lemon juice and toss well. Season to taste.

Serve with lemon halves, pitta bread and other Lebanese mezze dishes.

125 g bulgar wheat

2 large ripe red tomatoes

a bunch of flat leaf parsley

a large bunch of mint

3 spring onions, sliced

2 tablespoons fruity olive oil

1 tablespoon freshly squeezed lemon juice

sea salt and cracked black pepper

SERVES 4

VEGETABLES

Pumpkin oil is a favourite of mine, dark green, toasty and nutty – and you need far less than any other oil. It's supposed to be good for you, but frankly it tastes so good that I wouldn't mind if it were as sinful as chocolate. If you can't find it, omit from this salad and make the dressing without it. Microwaving green vegetables keeps them crisp and green, but you can also steam or blanch them.

Green vegetable salad
with pumpkin oil dressing

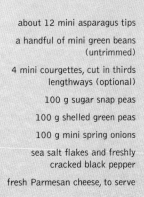

about 12 mini asparagus tips

a handful of mini green beans (untrimmed)

4 mini courgettes, cut in thirds lengthways (optional)

100 g sugar snap peas

100 g shelled green peas

100 g mini spring onions

sea salt flakes and freshly cracked black pepper

fresh Parmesan cheese, to serve

PUMPKIN OIL DRESSING

6 parts extra virgin olive oil

1 part Japanese rice vinegar or white wine vinegar

½ teaspoon Dijon mustard

a little sea salt and freshly cracked black pepper

pumpkin oil

SERVES 4

Microwave the asparagus tips, beans, courgettes, sugar snaps and green peas separately on HIGH for 2 minutes each, then transfer immediately to a bowl of ice cubes and water. This stops them cooking and sets the colour.

To make the dressing, put the olive oil, vinegar, mustard, salt and pepper in a screw-top jar and shake well to form an emulsion. Put in a bowl, add the drained vegetables, one kind at a time, and toss until lightly coated. Arrange the asparagus, courgettes and spring onions on a serving platter or 4 rectangular salad plates. Add the sugar snaps and green peas, then sprinkle with pumpkin oil (you don't need much - its flavour is very assertive). Shave fresh Parmesan over the top and sprinkle with sea salt flakes and cracked black pepper.

Alter the vegetable components of this salad according to what's in season. Try broccoli or carrots sliced lengthways into matchsticks, spinach leaves, sliced Chinese cabbage or cauliflower florets. I like snake beans rather than ordinary beans for salads, because they keep their crunch better.

Indonesian gado-gado

2 mini cucumbers, such as Lebanese, halved lengthways and deseeded

8 snake beans, cut into 5 cm lengths

1 orange or red pepper

2 firm tofu cakes

20–25 prawn crackers

2 onions, finely sliced into rings

a large handful of beansprouts, rinsed, drained and trimmed

2 heads Little Gem lettuce

15 cm daikon (white radish or mooli), peeled and grated

2 hard-boiled eggs, quartered

sea salt flakes

peanut oil, for frying

PEANUT SAUCE

250 g shelled fresh peanuts

2 red chillies, halved, deseeded and finely chopped

2 bird's eye chillies, halved, deseeded and finely chopped

1 onion, finely chopped

1 garlic clove, crushed

1 teaspoon sea salt

2 teaspoons brown sugar

200 ml coconut milk

SERVES 4

To make the peanut sauce, toast the peanuts in a dry frying pan. Transfer to a tea towel, rub off the skins, then put the nuts in a blender. Grind to a coarse meal, then add the chillies, onion, garlic, salt, sugar and coconut milk. Blend to a purée, then transfer to a saucepan and cook, stirring, until thickened.

Finely slice the halved cucumbers diagonally, put on a plate, sprinkle with salt, let stand for 10 minutes, then rinse and pat dry with kitchen paper. Chill.

Cook the snake beans in boiling salted water until *al dente*, then drain, rinse immediately under cold running water, then transfer to a bowl of iced water. Just before serving, drain again and pat dry with kitchen paper.

Peel the pepper with a vegetable peeler, cut off and discard the top and bottom, then halve, deseed and finely slice lengthways.

Heat 2 tablespoons of the peanut oil in a frying pan, add the tofu and cook until brown on both sides, then drain and slice thickly.

To cook the prawn crackers, fill a wok one-third full with peanut oil and heat to 190°C (375°F). Drop in one cracker to test the temperature – it should puff up immediately. Add the crackers, crowding them so they curl up, then cook until puffed and golden, about 3 seconds. Remove and drain on kitchen paper.

To cook the onion rings, reheat the oil, add the sliced onion and deep-fry until crisp and golden. Remove and drain on kitchen paper.

Arrange the cucumbers, snake beans, pepper, tofu, beansprouts, lettuce, daikon and quartered eggs on a large platter. Top with the onion rings and crackers, drizzle with the peanut sauce, sprinkle with salt and serve.

Warm roasted vegetable salad
with goats' cheese and pesto

Gorgeous with your choice of roasted vegetables. My favourite is pumpkin — and I also include tomatoes to act as a sauce.

2 red and 2 yellow peppers, halved and deseeded

500 g green-skinned pumpkin, peeled, but with seeds intact, cut into 3 cm wedges

2 sweet potatoes, cut into 3 cm chunks

2 red onions, quartered lengthways into wedges

125 ml extra virgin olive oil, plus extra for brushing and drizzling

a handful of basil leaves

4 cherry tomatoes, halved

8 teaspoons pesto (page 61)

about 100 g mature goats' cheese, cut into 8 chunks

4 medium tomatoes, halved

sea salt flakes and freshly ground black pepper

lemon wedges, to serve

SERVES 4–6

Put all the vegetables except the tomatoes in a plastic bag, add the olive oil, salt and pepper, then shake until everything is well coated in oil.

Brush a roasting tin with more oil and add the peppers, cut side up. Put a basil leaf, a halved cherry tomato, a spoonful of pesto and a chunk of goats' cheese in each pepper half. Drizzle more olive oil over the top.

Add the pumpkin, sweet potatoes, red onions and medium tomatoes, leaving space around each piece (use 2 roasting tins if necessary).

Put the tin or tins in an oven preheated to the highest possible temperature, at least 200°C (400°F) Gas 6, but as high as your oven will go. Roast for 30 minutes or until all the vegetables are tender and crispy brown at the edges.

Serve with extra fresh basil leaves and wedges of lemon. Toasted or char-grilled ciabatta or focaccia is also delicious. A hands-on dish.

Three potato salad
with chives and parsley

500 g small blue potatoes

500 g baby red potatoes

500 g baby yellow
or white potatoes

1 tablespoon olive oil

a bunch of flat leaf parsley,
leaves finely chopped

a bunch of chives, scissor-snipped

VINAIGRETTE

5 tablespoons extra virgin olive oil
(the best you can find)

1 tablespoon sherry vinegar

1 teaspoon Dijon mustard

sea salt and freshly ground
black pepper

SERVES 4

Put all the vinaigrette ingredients in a screw-top jar and shake until emulsified – put more salt in the dressing than usual, since you will have steamed the potatoes rather than boiling them in salted water.

Steam all the potatoes until tender, with the skins just beginning to split. (I steam them in separate layers of a bamboo steamer, since they are inclined to cook at different rates.) Dunk immediately into iced water to cool. Cut the blue potatoes in half and slip off the skins (this will show off the colour better).

Drain the red and yellow or white potatoes and pat dry with kitchen paper. Put 1 tablespoon of olive oil in a bowl, add all the potatoes and toss gently to coat. Transfer to a salad bowl, drizzle with the vinaigrette and sprinkle with parsley and chives.

I love this salad because I absolutely adore the smoky, earthy taste of blue potatoes. They have a very short season and can be hard to find, but, if you do, make a fuss of them like this. If unavailable, use extra potatoes of either of the other colours.

Tuscan panzanella

There are as many variations of this Tuscan bread salad as there are cooks. The trick is to let the flavours blend well without allowing the bread to disintegrate into a mush. Always use the ripest, reddest, most flavourful tomatoes you can find – sweet 'marmande', with its furrowed skin, is my favourite variety.

6 very ripe plum or marmande tomatoes

2 garlic cloves, sliced into slivers

4 thick slices day-old bread, preferably Italian-style such as pugliese or ciabatta

about 10 cm cucumber, halved, deseeded and finely sliced diagonally

1 red onion, diced

1 tablespoon chopped fresh flat leaf parsley

8–12 tablespoons extra virgin olive oil

2 tablespoons white wine vinegar, cider vinegar or sherry vinegar

1 teaspoon balsamic vinegar (optional)

a bunch of basil, leaves torn

12 caperberries or 4 tablespoons capers packed in brine, rinsed and drained

sea salt and freshly ground black pepper

SERVES 4

Cut the tomatoes in half, spike with slivers of garlic and roast in a preheated oven at 180°C (350°F) Gas 4 for about 1 hour, or until wilted and some of the moisture has evaporated.

Meanwhile, put the bread on an oiled stove-top grill pan and cook until lightly toasted and barred with grill marks on both sides. Tear or cut the toast into pieces and put into a salad bowl. Sprinkle with a little water until damp.

Add the tomatoes, cucumber, onion, parsley, salt and pepper. Sprinkle with the olive oil and vinegar, toss well, then set aside for about 1 hour to develop the flavours.

Add the basil leaves and caperberries or capers and serve.

FISH CHICKEN AND MEAT

Smoked salmon salad

250 g shelled broad beans, fresh or frozen

12 baby red potatoes

4–5 tablespoons extra virgin olive oil

100 g smoked salmon, diced`

a handful of fresh chives, scissor-snipped

4 teaspoons cider vinegar, white wine vinegar or rice vinegar

sea salt flakes and cracked black pepper

SERVES 4

The salty, smoky taste of salmon blends well with the starchy texture of potatoes. Broad beans are one of the few foods that don't seem to suffer from the freezing process. In fact, since they're frozen almost as soon as they're picked, their texture can often be better than those you buy at the market – fresh ones might have been harvested days earlier and their natural sweetness turns to starch very quickly after picking. Like most green vegetables, broad beans are very good cooked in a microwave.

Microwave the broad beans on HIGH for 3 minutes if fresh or 2 minutes if frozen. Transfer immediately to a bowl of iced water. When cold, pop them out of their grey skins, discard the skins and reserve the beans.

Boil the potatoes whole in their skins until tender, about 15–20 minutes (the time depends on the size of the potatoes). Drain, then toss in 2-3 teaspoons of the olive oil (gently so as not to break the skins). Cut the potatoes in half and arrange on 4 chilled plates. Top with the broad beans and diced smoked salmon. Sprinkle with sea salt flakes, cracked black pepper and scissor-snipped chives. Drizzle with about 1 tablespoon of extra virgin olive oil per plate and sprinkle with 1 teaspoon rice vinegar. Serve.

Salade niçoise

10 baby red potatoes

8 quails' eggs

100 g shelled broad beans, fresh or frozen, or 6 cooked baby artichokes, halved

100 g green beans, topped and tailed

3 spring onions, halved lengthways

2 small red onions, halved lengthways

1 mini cucumber, unwaxed

2 red or yellow peppers, peeled (see method)

4 Little Gem baby lettuces

1 punnet cherry tomatoes, about 20, halved

1 small can anchovy fillets or tuna, drained

about 20 Provençal black olives, pitted

about 20 caperberries or 3 tablespoons salt-packed capers, rinsed and drained

a large handful of fresh basil leaves

olive oil, for tossing

VINAIGRETTE

6 tablespoons extra virgin olive oil

1 tablespoon white wine vinegar, cider vinegar or sherry vinegar

1 teaspoon Dijon mustard (optional)

1 garlic clove, crushed

sea salt and freshly ground black pepper

SERVES 4 AS A STARTER,
8 AS A MAIN COURSE

Cook the baby potatoes in boiling salted water until tender, about 10 minutes. Drain and plunge them into a bowl of iced water with ice cubes. Let cool. Drain, then toss in a little olive oil and cut in half.

Boil the quails' eggs for 1½ minutes, then drain and plunge into cold water. Peel in a bowl of cold water. (They can be difficult to peel: you need to crack the shell and also pierce the very tough skin underneath. The water will help separate the skin.) Cut in half just before serving.

Microwave the broad beans on HIGH for 3 minutes if fresh or 2 minutes if frozen. Plunge into iced water, then pop each bean out of its grey skin. Microwave the green beans for 2 minutes, then plunge into iced water. Alternatively, steam the broad beans and green beans until tender.

Blanch the spring onions for 30 seconds in boiling water. Drain and plunge into the iced water.

Finely slice the onions and cucumber, preferably on a mandoline - slice the cucumber diagonally. If peeling the peppers, do so using a vegetable peeler, then cut into thick strips.

Put the lettuce leaves on a platter. Make bundles of blanched green beans and tie up with blanched spring onion leaves. Add the potatoes, quails' eggs, tomatoes, cucumber, onions and pepper. Top with anchovy fillets or tuna, black olives, caperberries or capers and basil leaves. Mix the vinaigrette ingredients in a small jug and serve separately.

A wonderful lunch for four or a starter for eight. Choose small, delicious and interesting potatoes – or leave them out. Quails' eggs are pretty and fun, instead of the usual hens' eggs. Use your choice of the other ingredients: the basics are the anchovies or tuna, plus the beans, lettuce, tomatoes, olives and onions.

Thai spicy shrimp salad

This salad is very simple – you can also make it with pre-cooked prawns. When preparing the lemongrass and kaffir lime leaves, make sure to slice them very finely indeed. If you can't find them, use a squeeze of lemon juice and some grated lime zest instead.

1 tablespoon peanut oil

12 uncooked prawns, shelled, deveined and halved lengthways

1 stalk lemongrass, very finely chopped

a handful of fresh coriander leaves, finely chopped

2 pink Thai shallots or 1 small regular shallot, finely sliced lengthways

3 spring onions, finely chopped

1 red chilli, finely sliced and deseeded if preferred

2 kaffir lime leaves, mid-rib removed, the leaves very finely sliced crossways, then finely chopped

12 cherry tomatoes, halved

a handful of mint sprigs, to serve

THAI DRESSING

4 tablespoons fish sauce

juice of 1 lemon or 2 limes

2 teaspoons brown sugar

2 tablespoons red Thai curry paste

SERVES 4

Heat the oil in a wok, add the prawns and stir-fry for about 1 minute until opaque. Let cool.

Put the dressing ingredients in a bowl and beat well with a fork until the sugar dissolves. Add the prawns and all the other ingredients, except the mint sprigs. Toss, then serve, topped with mint.

Vietnamese chicken salad

4 handfuls of beansprouts, rinsed and drained

1 young carrot

6 spring onions, halved, then finely sliced lengthways

a handful of fresh mint leaves, preferably Vietnamese mint

a handful of Asian basil leaves (optional)

2 tablespoons roasted peanuts, finely chopped

POACHED CHICKEN

2 chicken breasts, on the bone

2.5 cm fresh ginger, sliced

1 garlic clove, crushed

1 tablespoon fish sauce or a pinch of salt

1 red chilli, sliced

2 spring onions, sliced

boiling chicken stock or water, to cover

CHILLI-LIME DRESSING

75 ml freshly squeezed lime juice, about 2–3 limes

1 tablespoon fish sauce

2 tablespoons brown sugar

1 green chilli, halved, deseeded and finely chopped

1 red chilli, halved, deseeded and finely chopped

1 garlic clove, crushed

2.5 cm fresh ginger, peeled and grated

SERVES 4

You can use any cooked chicken for this salad. However, poaching is a very healthy way of cooking: there is no added fat, and much of what's there melts away as the chicken cooks. This salad isn't authentic – that would involve stir-fried chicken mince – but it's easy and it tastes fresh and good, like most Vietnamese food. If you can't find Vietnamese mint and Asian basil, you can substitute ordinary mint, but not ordinary basil (just leave it out).

Put the chicken in a wide saucepan, add the ginger, garlic, fish sauce or salt, chilli and spring onions. Add chicken stock or water to cover and return to the boil. Reduce the heat, cover with a lid and simmer, without boiling, until the chicken is tender, about 15–20 minutes. Remove from the heat and let cool in the liquid. Remove from the liquid, take the meat off the bone, discard bone and skin, then pull the chicken into long shreds. Reserve the cooking liquid for another use, such as soup.

Mix all the dressing ingredients in a screw-top jar and shake to mix.

To trim the beansprouts, pinch off the tails and remove the bean from between the two leaves (optional).

To prepare the carrot, peel and shred into long matchsticks on a mandoline or the large blade of a box grater.

Pile the beansprouts on 4 plates. Add the carrot and chicken and top with the spring onions, mint and basil leaves, if using. Sprinkle with the dressing and roasted peanuts, then serve.

Insalata gonzaga

A marvellous, simple chicken salad named after
the Gonzagas, who were the Dukes of Mantua, near
Modena, the home of balsamic vinegar. True balsamic
vinegar is rare and expensive, but use the best you can
afford. This recipe comes from my young Italian
cousin who can turn out utterly delicious dishes
seemingly without effort.

100 g pine nuts

6 tablespoons extra virgin olive oil,
preferably from Tuscany or Umbria

1 tablespoon wine vinegar,
red or white

500 g skinless, boneless,
roasted chicken breasts

2 small red radicchio lettuces,
leaves separated

4 tablespoons raisins*

1–2 tablespoons balsamic vinegar

sea salt and freshly cracked
black pepper

100 g fresh Parmesan cheese at
room temperature, cut into shards,
to serve

SERVES 4

Put the pine nuts in a dry frying pan
and heat, stirring, until lightly golden.
Remove to a plate.

Put the oil and vinegar in a salad bowl,
add a pinch of salt and beat with a
fork. Slice the chicken or pull it into
shreds. Add the chicken and radicchio
to the bowl and toss gently.

Serve on salad plates, sprinkle with
the raisins, pepper and balsamic
vinegar and top with shards of
Parmesan.

Note: For this salad, I soaked the raisins in
verjuice for 10 minutes before adding to the
salad. Verjuice is halfway between vinegar
and wine – delicious, if a little difficult to
find. Omit if necessary.

Rare beef salad
with parsley oil and wasabi mayonnaise

A splendid special-occasion salad for a summer lunch party. When you serve it, cut slices of beef about 1 cm wide – there's nothing worse than mean little paper-thin slices – it always looks as though you bought them at a cheap sandwich bar. For the best flavour, let the meat return to room temperature before serving (it only takes a few minutes). Increase the amount of fillet to cater for the number of guests – since it's the same thickness, it will take the same amount of time in the oven, no matter how big it is.

1 beef fillet, about 50 cm long, well trimmed

250 g peppery leaves, such as watercress, wild rocket or, when in season, wild garlic (rampion)

sea salt and freshly ground black pepper

olive oil, for sealing

PARSLEY OIL

a bunch of parsley

250 ml extra virgin olive oil

WASABI MAYONNAISE

250 ml homemade mayonnaise (page 62)

2–3 tablespoons wasabi paste (about 1 tube)

SERVES 12

To make the parsley oil, put the parsley and olive oil in a blender and blend until smooth. Set aside for 30 minutes or overnight in the refrigerator.

Brush a heavy-based roasting tin with olive oil and heat on top of the stove until very hot. Add the beef and seal on all sides until nicely browned. Transfer to a preheated oven and roast at 200°C (400°F) Gas 6 for 20 minutes. Remove from the oven and set aside to fix the juices. Sprinkle with salt and pepper.

Let the meat cool to room temperature and reserve any cooking juices. If preparing in advance, wrap closely in foil and chill, but return it and the parsley oil to room temperature before serving.

Arrange the leaves down the middle of a rectangular or oval serving dish. Slice the beef into 1 cm thick slices with a very sharp carving knife (or an electric knife). Arrange in overlapping slices on top of the leaves and pour any cooking juices from the roasting tin or carving board over the top.

Drizzle the parsley oil, strained if necessary, over the beef. Mix the mayonnaise with the wasabi paste and serve separately.

BEANS GRAINS AND NOODLES

Quick couscous salad

This very quick and easy salad is endlessly adaptable, and great if you want to take your lunch to work. I prefer wholegrain couscous, but use regular if you like. Easy-cook couscous is supposed to be just soaked then drained, but I find it's better for a little more steaming or microwaving after soaking.

4 tablespoons easy-cook wholegrain couscous

125 ml boiling chicken stock or water

1 cooked chicken breast, pulled into shreds

3 halves sun-blushed (semi-dried) tomatoes or 6 fresh cherry tomatoes, halved

2 marinated artichoke hearts, sliced

3–4 spring onions, sliced

400 g canned chickpeas, rinsed and drained

2–3 tablespoons extra virgin olive oil or 1 tablespoon pumpkin oil

1 teaspoon white rice vinegar or wine vinegar

1 teaspoon Dijon mustard (optional)

sea salt and freshly ground black pepper

a handful of flat leaf parsley, coarsely chopped, or a few sprigs of watercress

SERVES 2

Put the couscous in a non-metal jug or bowl and cover with the stock or water. Leave for 15 minutes until the water has been absorbed. For a fluffier texture, put the soaked couscous in a strainer and steam over simmering water for another 10 minutes, or microwave in the jug or bowl on 50 per cent for about 5 minutes. Drain if necessary, pressing the liquid through the strainer with a spoon. Let cool.

When ready to make up the salad, put a layer of couscous in a lidded plastic container, then add a layer of chicken. Add the tomatoes, artichoke hearts, spring onions and chickpeas. Keep the leaves in a separate container until just before serving.

Put the oil in a screw-top jar, add the vinegar, mustard, if using, salt and pepper and mix well. Sprinkle over the salad. Cover and carry.

To serve, add the parsley and watercress and toss well.

Tonno e fagioli
Italian tuna and beans

1 large tuna steak, about 250 g,
or 2 small cans good-quality tuna,
about 160 g each, drained

6 tablespoons olive oil, plus extra for brushing

2 red onions, finely sliced

2–3 fat garlic cloves, crushed

1 tablespoon sherry vinegar or
white wine vinegar

1 kg cooked or canned green flageolet beans,
white cannellini beans, or a mixture of both

4 handfuls of fresh basil leaves
and small sprigs

sea salt and freshly ground black pepper

SERVES 6 AS A STARTER,
4 AS A MAIN COURSE

I first tasted this dish in a restaurant on the edge of the piazza in Siena with my 10-year-old Italian cousin. White cannellini beans are usual, but I like the taste and pretty colour of green flageolets. Fresh tuna can be expensive, so this recipe is a good way of making one wonderful steak stretch a little further.

If using fresh tuna, brush with olive oil and put on a preheated stove-top grill pan. Cook for 3 minutes on each side or until barred with brown but pink in the middle (the time depends on the thickness of the fish). Remove from the pan, cool and pull into chunks.

Put the oil, onions, crushed garlic and vinegar in a bowl and beat with a fork. Add the beans and toss until well coated.

Add the tuna and basil, salt and pepper, then serve with crusty bread and Italian red wine.

Vietnamese table salad
with herbs, vegetables and noodles

A do-it-yourself salad platter is served with every Vietnamese meal. Some people think the idea was borrowed from the French, but in fact it is indigenous. The combinations of vegetables are almost infinite and the herbs give a fresh, scented flavour. To eat, take a lettuce leaf from the platter, add your choice of herbs and other ingredients, then wrap the leaf into a parcel and dip in the spicy sauce.

2 teaspoons white rice vinegar

2 teaspoons sugar

½ teaspoon sea salt

2 large carrots, cut into matchstick strips

about 20 cm cucumber, halved lengthways

60 g beanthread noodles (optional)

4 Little Gem lettuces or 1 iceberg lettuce, leaves separated

6 spring onions, shredded

a handful of beansprouts, rinsed and trimmed

a large bunch of coriander

a large bunch of mint, leaves only

a bunch of Asian basil – not sweet basil, leaves only (optional)

NUÓC CHAM DIPPING SAUCE

2 garlic cloves, crushed

1 red chilli, deseeded and chopped

1 tablespoon brown sugar

juice of ½ lime

4 tablespoons fish sauce

1 small red or green chilli, sliced, to serve

SERVES 4

Put the vinegar, sugar and salt in a bowl, add 250 ml water and the strips of carrot, stir well and set aside for 30 minutes or up to 24 hours. Drain.

Finely slice the cucumber halves diagonally into half-moons.

If using noodles, bring a large saucepan of water to the boil, add the noodles and stir to separate. Boil for 2 minutes, then drain and transfer to a bowl of iced water until ready to use.

To make the Nuóc Cham, mash the garlic, chilli and sugar with a mortar and pestle to form a paste. Stir in the lime juice, fish sauce and 4 tablespoons water. Taste and add extra water if preferred and put into a small dipping bowl. Add the sliced chilli.

Arrange the lettuce leaves in the middle of a large serving platter, then put piles of drained carrot, cucumber, spring onions, beansprouts and herbs around the outside. Drain the noodles, if using, and put in a separate bowl.

To eat, take a lettuce leaf, add your choice of other ingredients, then roll up. Dip in the *Nuóc Cham* and eat.

Soba noodles, made from buckwheat, are wonderful cold, served on flat baskets or in slatted wooden boxes. Other Japanese noodles, such as white somen noodles or the larger, ribbon-like udon, are also delicious served this way. I particularly like the beautiful green-tea-flavoured, pale green, cha-soba noodles ('cha' means 'tea' in many languages).

Japanese soba noodle salad

400 g dried soba noodles

12 dried shiitake mushrooms

2 tablespoons Japanese soy sauce

2 tablespoons mirin
(Japanese rice wine) or sherry

12 uncooked prawns

12 spring onions, finely sliced

4 teaspoons furokaki pepper (optional)

4 teaspoons wasabi paste, to serve

DIPPING SAUCE

250 ml dashi stock*

2 tablespoons mirin

a pinch of sugar

3 tablespoons Japanese soy sauce

SERVES 4

*Dashi stock is available in powder or concentrate form in Chinese and Japanese shops. Dissolve 1 teaspoon in 1 cup hot (not boiling) water, or to taste.

Put the dipping sauce ingredients in a saucepan, simmer for about 5 minutes, then chill.

Cook the noodles for 5–6 minutes or according to the packet instructions. Drain, rinse in cold water and cool over ice. Chill.

Put the shiitakes in a saucepan, cover with 250 ml boiling water and soak until soft. Remove and discard the mushroom stems. Add the soy sauce and mirin to the pan, bring to the boil and simmer for a few minutes to meld the flavours. Add the prawns and simmer for about 1 minute until firm. Drain, reserving the cooking liquid. Shell the prawns, but leave the tail fins intact. Devein and split each prawn down the back to the fin, giving a butterfly shape. Chill the prawns and poaching liquid. Just before serving, dunk the chilled noodles in the liquid, then drain.

To serve, put a layer of ice cubes in a slatted wooden box or bowl, then add the noodles. Add the prawns, spring onions and mushrooms. Sprinkle with furokaki pepper, if using. Serve with separate dishes of wasabi paste and dipping sauce.

Chickpea lunchbox salad

Chickpeas are the basis of my favourite lunchbox salads. You can part-prepare them, so the dressing soaks into the chickpeas, then add the fresh ingredients just before serving. You can add any number of other ingredients, including olives, Parma ham, salami or chorizo, canned tuna, other vegetables, leaves or herbs, and a few of your favourite spices. Whatever takes your fancy in your Italian deli.

1 kg cooked or canned chickpeas, rinsed and drained

250 g marinated artichoke hearts

250 g sun-blushed (semi-dried) tomatoes (optional)

250 g very ripe cherry tomatoes, halved

8 spring onions, finely sliced diagonally

leaves from 8 sprigs of basil, torn

a small bunch of chives, scissor-snipped

leaves from 4 sprigs of flat leaf parsley, chopped

50 g fresh Parmesan, shaved

1 tablespoon black pepper, cracked with a mortar and pestle

DRESSING

6 tablespoons extra virgin olive oil

1 tablespoon freshly squeezed lemon juice or sherry vinegar

1 teaspoon Dijon mustard (optional)

1 small garlic clove, crushed

sea salt and freshly ground black pepper

SERVES 4

Put the dressing ingredients in a screw-top jar and shake well.

Put the chickpeas, artichoke hearts and sun-blushed tomatoes, if using, in a bowl or lunchbox. Pour over the dressing. Cover with a lid and chill for up to 4 hours.

When ready to serve, add the cherry tomatoes, spring onions, basil, chives and parsley. Stir gently, then sprinkle with the shaved Parmesan and pepper.

Note: Sun-blushed tomatoes, which are partially-dried sun-dried tomatoes, are sold in Italian gourmet stores.

FRUITS

Watermelon and feta salad
with ginger and chillies

I adore watermelons — they were a school picnic treat where I grew up and they have never lost their romance in my eyes. I love them by themselves, in crushes and smoothies — and also as a savoury salad with salty cheese and cracked pepper.

4 thick slices watermelon

250 g feta cheese or
125 g Parmesan

1 tablespoon black
peppercorns

3 cm fresh ginger, peeled

juice of 1 lime

2 tablespoons nut oil
or extra virgin olive oil

1 red chilli, deseeded
and finely sliced

sea salt flakes

SERVES 4

Cut the watermelon slices into triangular wedges and remove the seeds. Cut the feta cheese into long shards or crumble into large pieces. If using Parmesan, shave it into long pieces with a vegetable peeler. Coarsely crush the peppercorns. Grate the ginger and squeeze the juice from the gratings into a small jug (you can also press it through a garlic crusher). Add the lime juice and oil and beat with a fork.

Arrange the watermelon pieces on a plate or in a bowl, standing them vertically. Add the feta or Parmesan, crushed peppercorns and a little salt. Sprinkle with the ginger dressing and sliced chilli, then serve.

Asian pear salad
with macadamias and macadamia nut oil

Toast the sesame seeds in a dry frying pan for about 1 minute, stirring, until lightly golden. Set aside.

Blanch the beans in boiling water for 3 minutes or until *al dente*. Remove and plunge into iced water. Let cool, then drain and pat dry. Put the olive oil in a bowl, then add the beans, chillies and leaves. Toss gently to coat.

Slice the pears into wedges, cut off the cores, then brush the wedges with the lime juice. Add to the bowl and toss gently to coat.

Arrange piles of the dressed salad on 4 small plates. Sprinkle with the nuts, sesame seeds, sea salt and black pepper. Drizzle with macadamia oil and serve.

1 tablespoon white sesame seeds

100 g snake beans (Chinese long beans), cut into 5 cm lengths, or French beans

1 tablespoon extra virgin olive oil

2 red chillies, finely sliced

about 100 g wild rocket leaves

about 250 g other salad leaves

2 Asian pears or 4 red-skinned pears

juice of 1 lime

100 g macadamia nuts, preferably unroasted and unsalted

4 tablespoons macadamia nut oil

sea salt and freshly ground black pepper

SERVES 4

Macadamia nuts are native to Queensland, Australia, and since I am too, this salad is in honour of my home state. You can use your favourite nuts: but try to match nut and oil, hazelnuts and hazelnut oil, or walnuts and walnut oil. Keep nut oils in the fridge, because they are very delicate and can go rancid very quickly (as can the nuts themselves, so keep them there too).

Papaya salsa

Serve this fresh and juicy salad with kebabs of char-grilled tuna, poached chicken or barbecued meats. It's also terrific with tortilla or pitta wraps. I like papaya, but you could use other fruits instead – like avocado, apple or nashi pear (brushed with lemon juice to stop them browning), or perhaps pineapple or watermelon.

1 medium papaya, about 250 g
1 red and 1 yellow pepper
3 cm fresh ginger, peeled and grated
1 red chilli, deseeded and diced
6 baby cornichons, finely sliced
6 tablespoons torn fresh coriander leaves
grated zest and juice of 3 limes
sea salt and freshly ground black pepper

SERVES 4–6

Peel the papaya with a vegetable peeler, cut it in half lengthways and scoop out the seeds, then dice the flesh and put in a bowl.

Peel the peppers with a vegetable peeler, deseed and dice. Add to the bowl, then add the ginger, diced chilli and cornichons. Stir in the coriander, lime zest and juice, and set aside for about 10 minutes to develop the flavours.

Serve with meat, fish or poultry.

Moroccan orange salad
with mint, harissa and red onion

Variations of this Moroccan classic can be made with
orange flower water in the dressing, or with crushed
cardamom instead of cinnamon, or nutmeg and cloves.
Make sure you cut off all the white pith from the orange
before slicing – the pith is very bitter and spoils the salad.

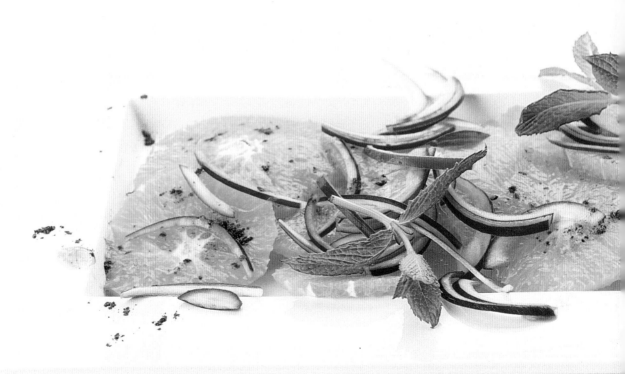

3 oranges

1 red onion, halved lengthways, then finely sliced into narrow wedges

a handful of mint sprigs

1 teaspoon ground cinnamon or mild chilli powder

ORANGE DRESSING

juice from the oranges (see method)

2 tablespoons fruity extra virgin olive oil

1 teaspoon harissa paste

sea salt and freshly ground black pepper

SERVES 4

Grate the zest of 1 of the oranges and put in a bowl. Cut a thick slice off the top and bottom of each orange. Squeeze the juice out of the tops and bottoms and add to the bowl. Set the fruit flat on a cutting board. With a very sharp knife, cut off the orange peel in sections from top to bottom, making sure you remove all the white pith. Slice the oranges thinly crossways, saving any juice and pouring it into the bowl. Squeeze the juice from 1–2 slices and add it to the bowl.

Arrange the orange slices on a flat plate, top with the onion and mint sprigs and sprinkle with cinnamon or chilli powder.

Add the olive oil, harissa paste, salt and pepper to the bowl of orange juice, mix well, sprinkle over the salad, then serve.

To make the dressing, put all the ingredients in a saucepan, add 250 ml water, bring to the boil and simmer until the sugar has dissolved and the liquid is a light syrup. Remove from the heat and let cool.

Peel the papaya with a vegetable peeler, cut in half lengthways and remove and discard the seeds. Cut the flesh into large dice. Put in a bowl with any juice.

Cut the top and bottom off the pineapple, stand it on its base, then slice off the skin. Remove all the prickly eyes. Cut the pineapple into 4 wedges, then slice off the cores. Cut 1 of the wedges into bite-size triangles. Add to the bowl with any juice. Crush the remaining pineapple in a blender or juicer and add to the bowl.

Open the passionfruit and scrape into the salad.

Add your choice of the other fruit, but reserve the bananas until later. Sprinkle with the dressing and chill for at least 1 hour. When ready to serve, slice in the banana and serve with crème fraîche or ice cream.

1 large ripe papaya, about 40 cm long, or several smaller ones

1 ripe pineapple

6 ripe passionfruit (with wrinkled skin)

2 ripe bananas

other tropical fruits, as available, such as; nashi pears, roseapples, kiwifruit, prickly pear fruit, pink guavas, lychees, longans or pomelo segments, all prepared as required

crème fraîche or ice cream, to serve

THAI GINGER DRESSING

250 g sugar, brown or granulated

grated zest and juice of 3 limes or 1 lemon

3 cm fresh ginger, peeled and grated

SERVES 4 OR MORE

Tropical fruit salad
with Thai ginger dressing

I grew up in sub-tropical Australia, so I think that fruit salad should always be based on tropical fruits, especially pineapple and papaya. Choose whatever is available where you live, but include at least some tropicals. Some fruits, such as bananas, go 'furry' in juice, so should be added at the last minute. If you prefer a clearer sauce, make the ginger dressing with white sugar rather than brown.

DRESSINGS

Pesto

125 ml extra virgin olive oil

4 tablespoons pine nuts

6 garlic cloves, crushed

1 teaspoon sea salt

a large bunch of fresh basil leaves, torn

50 g freshly grated Parmesan cheese

50 g freshly grated pecorino cheese

MAKES ABOUT 250 ML

Brush a frying pan with a little of the olive oil, add the pine nuts and fry gently and quickly until golden (about 30 seconds). They burn very easily, so don't leave them. Let cool. Transfer to a food processor, add the garlic, salt and basil and blend to a paste. Add the Parmesan, blend again, then add the oil and pecorino and blend again until smooth.

CORIANDER PESTO

For a Middle Eastern flavour, omit the basil and use half parsley and half coriander. Omit the pine nuts and use almonds instead.

ROCKET PESTO

Use half parsley and half wild rocket leaves instead of the basil. Use all Parmesan instead of a mixture of cheeses.

PARSLEY PESTO

A much milder version using parsley instead of basil leaves.

RED PESTO

Instead of basil, use 250 g sun-blushed (semi-dried) tomatoes (or sun-dried tomatoes bottled in olive oil, but drained). A teaspoon of harissa paste lifts the flavour even further.

Asian dressings

Asian dressings are particularly delicious—and healthful because they often contain no oil. These include the Peanut Sauce (page 20), Chilli-Lime Dressing (page 34), Thai Dressing (page 32) and *Nuóc Cham* Dipping Sauce (page 45), which is also good as a dressing.

SESAME OIL DRESSING

3 cm fresh ginger, peeled and sliced

3 spring onions, chopped and quartered crossways

1 red chilli, deseeded and chopped

200 ml peanut oil (groundnut oil)

4 tablespoons sesame oil

1 tablespoon peppercorns, preferably Szechuan

Put the ginger, spring onions, chilli and peppercorns in a small blender and pulse to chop. Put the peanut and sesame oils in a saucepan and heat until hot but not smoking. Remove from the heat, add the flavourings, stir, cover with a lid, let cool, then strain. Serve tossed through blanched vegetables and with chicken or noodle salads. The dressing may also be marinated overnight before straining.

LIME DRESSING

1 tablespoon fish sauce

juice of 1 lime

1 teaspoon brown sugar

Mix in a small bowls and serve as a dipping sauce, or sprinkled over the salad.

Mayonnaise

The key to making mayonnaise is to have all the ingredients at room temperature, and to add the oil a few drops at a time at first, then more quickly, but not in a continuous stream as many books advise. The emulsion needs time to absorb the oil, so don't overtax it. Don't use all olive oil (unless you're making aioli) – the flavour is too strong. Use a light oil such as sunflower, but good quality: don't use those labelled just 'vegetable oil'. I use a food processor to make mayonnaise but, if you're a purist, by all means make it by hand.

2 egg yolks, at room temperature
1 whole egg (if making in a food processor)
2 teaspoons Dijon mustard
a large pinch of salt
2 teaspoons freshly squeezed lemon juice or white wine vinegar
250 ml good-quality sunflower, safflower or peanut oil (not corn oil)
125 ml virgin olive oil
MAKES ABOUT 2 CUPS

Put the eggs, mustard, salt and lemon juice in a food processor and blend until pale. Gradually add the oil, a few drops at a time at first, then more quickly, but in stages, leaving a few seconds between additions to allow the eggs to 'digest' the oil. When all the oil has been added, if the mixture is too thick, add about 1 tablespoon warm water. Serve immediately, or press a sheet of clingfilm over the surface to prevent a skin from forming. It may be refrigerated for up to 3 days.

AIOLI

An unctuous garlic mayonnaise served with Provençal dishes such as Salade Niçoise.

Crush 4 garlic cloves into a food processor at the same time as the eggs. Proceed as in the main recipe (use all olive oil if preferred).

Also delicious with 1 tablespoon harissa paste added (a quick version of rouille).

GREEN GODDESS DRESSING

Put 250 ml mayonnaise in a food processor. Add 50 g canned anchovies, salt, pepper, 2 tablespoons each of tarragon, parsley and chives, 1 tablespoon fresh lemonjuice and 3 tablespoons vinegar. Process until smooth.

Vinaigrette

5 tablespoons extra virgin olive oil

1 tablespoon white wine vinegar

1 teaspoon Dijon mustard (optional)

sea salt and freshly ground black pepper

MAKES ABOUT ½ CUP

Put all the ingredients in a salad bowl and beat with a fork or small whisk. Alternatively, put in a screw-top bottle and shake to form an emulsion.

VARIATIONS

I like to use Japanese rice vinegar, which gives a mild, smooth taste. You can also substitute red wine vinegar, sherry vinegar, cider vinegar, or others. Freshly squeezed lime or lemon juice are also traditional replacements for the vinegar.

A crushed garlic clove is often added to the vinaigrette. Delicious, but death to the breath.

Some people like to include a little sugar in the dressing. I think this is only necessary if you've used too much vinegar.

Instead of extra virgin, use 2 tablespoons mild virgin olive oil and 3 tablespoons nut oil such as walnut, macadamia, or hazelnut. Nut oils turn rancid very quickly, so buy small quantities, keep them in the refrigerator and use quickly (keep nuts there too).

A warm vinaigrette poured over salad leaves, meat, fish, or vegetables is also delicious.

One of the nicest dressings of all is just a sprinkle of the very best quality extra virgin olive oil.

index